EARTH UNDER ATTACK!

VOLCANO MELTS VILLAGE

Louise and Richard Spilsbury

Gareth Stevens
PUBLISHING

Please visit our website, **www.garethstevens.com**.
For a free color catalog of all our high-quality books,
call toll free 1-800-542-2595 of fax 1-877-542-2596.

Cataloging-in-Publication Data
Names: Spilsbury, Louise. | Spilsbury, Richard.
Title: Volcano melts village / Louise and Richard Spilsbury.
Description: New York : Gareth Stevens Publishing, 2018. | Series: Earth under attack! |
    Includes index.
Identifiers: ISBN 9781538213193 (pbk.) | ISBN 9781538213216 (library bound) |
    ISBN 9781538213209 (6 pack)
Subjects: LCSH: Volcanoes--Juvenile literature. | Natural disasters--Juvenile literature.
Classification: LCC QE521.3 S67 2018 | DDC 551.21--dc23

First Edition

Published in 2018 by
Gareth Stevens Publishing
111 East 14th Street, Suite 349
New York, NY 10003

Copyright © 2018 Gareth Stevens Publishing

Produced for Gareth Stevens by Calcium
Editors: Sarah Eason and Jennifer Sanderson
Designers: Jeni Child and Simon Borrough
Picture researcher: Rachel Blount

Picture credits: Cover: Shutterstock: Anton Ivanov center, BlackMac foreground, IKostiuchok top; Inside: Flickr:
European Commission DG ECHO: Mathias Eick EU/ECHO 32, USGS: 7, 40, 41; Shutterstock: Brisbane 35, George Burba
30, ChameleonsEye 44–45t, Chen WS 14, Robert Cicchetti 44, Matt Cooper 39, Designua 15, Peter Hermes Furian 8,
Aaron Galbusera 11, J. Helgason 33, Jubipulse34 19, KalypsoWorldPhotography 42, Alexey Kamenskiy 12, Khanbm52 17,
Sergey Krasnoshchokov 4–5t, F. Jimenez Meca 36–37t, MNStudio 12–13t, Byelikova Oksana 16, OverlandTheAmericas 6,
Vadim Petrakov 9, 24–25t, 31, Anton Petrus 21, Photovolcanica.com 26–27b, Pung 23, Dr Morley Read 24, TDway 29,
Saethapoeng Triechorb 10, Wead 22; Wikimedia Commons: Alpsdake 18, Crisco 1492 34, Eddyl 43, Chris Light 38, Xb-70
at English Wikipedia 26–27t.

Printed in China
CPSIA compliance information: Batch #CW18GS:
For further information contact Gareth Stevens, New York, New York at 1-800-542-2595.

CONTENTS

CHAPTER 1

VICIOUS VOLCANOES

Volcanoes are openings in Earth's surface. Most of the time, these openings are closed shut and barely noticeable. Then, suddenly, they can open and shoot out torrents of volcanic ash, gases, and viciously hot liquid rock. Eruptions like these can be violent and spectacular to witness. However, they can also be devastating, causing the tragic loss of many lives and huge amounts of damage and destruction for miles.

Underground Drama

The drama of a volcano starts deep underground. There, our planet is in motion, and different parts of the rock it is made from push against each other. Enormous forces and high temperatures build up from this pushing. They cause hot, liquid rock under high **pressure** to move around beneath the surface. The easiest places for it to escape the pressure are at the slightest gaps in the outer rocky skin of the Earth. It is at these places that volcanoes erupt.

Ingredients for Disaster

The bubbling rock, called lava, that bursts out from within Earth can spill down the sides of a volcano like burning hot syrup, or it can shoot into the air like a cork exploding from a bottle of soda. The clouds of gas and ash that billow out of a volcano and spread through the air can be hot, **dense**, and poisonous. Thick lava moves fairly slowly, allowing people to escape its path. On steep slopes, thinner lava can move more quickly, making it harder to get away.

A volcano in Russia spews out incredibly hot lava during a nighttime eruption.

Deadly Explosions

The name "volcano" comes from Roman times, when people named a volcanic island "Vulcan" after their god of fire. Soon, all volcanoes became known by this name. Many volcanoes are indeed characterized by a fiery glow and intense heat as red-hot lava pours out of them, burning anything in their paths to cinders. They may also spray large chunks of rock, splintered from the earth in the explosion, into the air. These can rain down like deadly missiles.

DEADLY DATA

The worst volcano ever recorded was Mount Tambora, Indonesia, in 1815. The lava and superheated gas flows killed many people. More people died in the following year because ash clouds blocked the sun and destroyed crops, causing famine. In total, the eruption killed almost 100,000 people.

Explosive Power

Most of the volcanic eruptions that occur are small and happen in volcanoes that are erupting gently most of the time. However, it is the other volcanoes people have to worry about: the rare enormous volcanoes. These explode violent blasts of ash, gas, and lava over nearby land and buildings, melting villages in their path.

Volcano Action

It is estimated that across the world at any time, there are around 20 volcanoes erupting, even right now as you read this sentence! Most of these will be small ones that cause minor clouds of ash. This ash can form a thin film of dust over cars and homes. Most of these eruptions will be unnoticed, partly because of their remote locations. Every year, there are a total of 50 to 70 volcanic eruptions. Volcanologists, the scientists who study volcanoes, believe that there are more than 500 volcanoes around the globe that could go off at some point in the future.

Vast clouds of heavy, hot, stinging ash are erupting from a volcano somewhere on Earth right now!

Volcanologists sometimes need to get dangerously close to volcanoes to study them.

Studying Volcanoes

Volcanologists are interested in knowing more about volcanoes. They study the processes involved in their formation, and when, how, and why they erupt. They study volcanic eruptions from the past and volcanoes that are erupting gently now. They try to figure out what combination of factors collide to result in the biggest, most disastrous eruptions. Then, they try to discover ways of getting better at predicting when a volcano is going to erupt. If scientists can predict these eruptions, they will be able to give people as much warning as possible, so that they can move out of the path of destruction.

EARTH UNDER ATTACK!

Volcanologists make new discoveries about volcanoes all the time, but it is still very difficult to predict exactly when a volcano will erupt until it is close to exploding. Volcanoes are dangerously unpredictable. Even volcanoes that have been peaceful for hundreds of years can one day spring to life again.

CHAPTER 2

WHAT LIES BENEATH

We live and move around Earth on solid ground. Whether muddy soil, sandy beach, or mountain ledge, all surfaces are on top of rock. However, we are actually floating on what lies beneath the solid rock.

Layer Upon Layer

If you could travel from the surface, deep into the center of Earth, you would discover that our planet is made up of layers. From surface to center, the four major layers are the crust, mantle, outer core, and inner core. The crust is made up of hard rock that is between 4 and 50 miles (6.4 and 80.4 km) deep in different places. Some crust is land, and some forms the floor of the oceans. Around 3 billion years ago, the outer part of our planet cracked and split into many pieces that fit together over the surface of the Earth, a lot like the panels on a soccer ball. These huge pieces of rock are called tectonic plates.

Tectonic Plates

Earth's tectonic plates are constantly shifting, but they do so incredibly slowly. They float on the lower, hottest parts of the mantle. This part of the mantle is partly melted, sticky rock. The mantle is constantly changing because the rock in it can melt into liquid called **magma**. Magma usually stays deep underground, but sometimes it reaches the surface. This usually happens at the weak points in the crust, which are the gaps between plates. Volcanoes are the places where magma escapes.

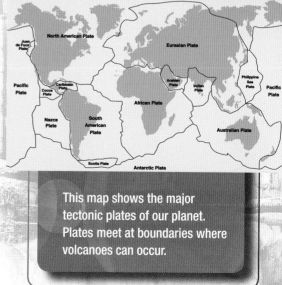

This map shows the major tectonic plates of our planet. Plates meet at boundaries where volcanoes can occur.

Red-hot magma cools to black rock at the Earth's surface. The outer part cools first, but the inner part can stay hot for much longer.

EARTH UNDER ATTACK!

The intense heat of Earth's core drives plate movements. The inner core is the hottest part of the planet. It is a ball of metal reaching 9,932° Fahrenheit (5,500° C). This keeps the outer core as liquid rock. The core heats up the mantle. Magma constantly rises nearer the surface and sinks back toward the core as it cools, creating a circular movement in the lower mantle. It is this movement that drags the plates along.

A Volcano Forms

Rising magma can be unstoppable. It reaches temperatures well above 1,652° Fahrenheit (900° C). This is hot enough to melt solid rock. The magma forces its way up from the depths, through weak parts or cracks in crust rock, or by melting tunnels through any solid rock blocking its path.

Mount Fuji is one of the most famous volcanoes on Earth. Its cone shape has grown over thousands of years of eruptions.

Pressure Release

Near the surface, the magma becomes stuck. The uppermost part cools and becomes thicker and less mobile, so the magma moves more slowly. The route for rising magma stays the same, so over time, more and more magma rises and becomes blocked. Sometimes, large bubbles of magma, called magma chambers, form. The trapped magma pushes with incredible force on the weak rock above. The pressure builds until finally, one day, it is too much. Then, the magma bursts through the crust as a volcanic eruption. Once it is at the surface, it is called lava.

Through a Volcano

If you had to draw a volcano, you would probably draw a triangle or cone shape. Some volcanoes do have this shape, but not all do. The cones are usually made up of layers of lava that have cooled and set. These layers started with the first eruption of the volcano, which left a small mound behind. Over time, the mound grew bigger with successive layers. The hole in the center top, where eruptions usually happen, is called the vent. However, lava can also ooze through the sides of volcano cones if magma melts horizontal tunnels through the rock. This is because this is an easier escape route for the lava than the vent. After an eruption happens, it can blast the top away around the vent. This hollowed out area is then called the crater.

DEADLY DATA

Some volcano cones grow over thousands of years, but others form in days. For example, in Paricutin, Mexico, in 1943, a farmer noticed a small mound in a cornfield. In a week, a volcano had grown five stories high; after a year, it had grown nearly 1,000 feet (305 m).

Volcanic craters form after rock near the vent is blasted away during violent eruptions. Some form lakes when rainwater collects there.

On Land or Under Sea

All volcanoes grow during an eruption, but they take on different shapes on the land's surface. Volcanoes can be tall, wide, big, or small.

Erupting Materials

The shape of the volcano depends partly on what erupts. Sometimes, magma breaks into tiny particles at the moment of eruption, rather than emerging as lava. The rock cap at the top of the volcano's vent shatters into tiny pieces, too. Tiny erupted pieces transform into gritty volcanic ash as they cool in the air. This ash, or cinder, rains down around the vent. Cinder cone volcanoes have small circular or oval cones formed from layers of ash.

Go with the Flow

A volcano's shape also depends on how the lava flows. Shield volcanoes have a shape like an upturned shield or bowl with very shallow slopes. These form when the lava is very runny because of the chemicals it contains. The lava spreads around evenly and affects a wide area. This contrasts with **lava domes**, where the erupting lava is thick and does not spread far from the vent. Cones are steeper than shield volcanoes.

Lava cools and sets quickly as it oozes into cool seawater.

The Hawaiian islands are lush today but were once bare rock growing up out of the Pacific Ocean depths after eruptions from a hot spot.

All at Sea

Some volcanoes are found underwater. They erupt and grow as they do on land, except that the lava cools quicker in the cold of the deep ocean. Over time, new islands can magically appear above the sea surface because of a recent eruption. They do not always grow over a fault where the edges of two plates meet. Sometimes, an island can appear over the middle of an ocean plate where the magma burns through. This is called a hot spot. As the plate shifts sideward, the hot spot stays put, and another island forms next to the first. The Hawaii Island chain in the Pacific Ocean formed in this way.

DEADLY DATA

The biggest volcano scientists know about is out of this world! It is Olympus Mons on planet Mars. This remarkable shield volcano is 17 miles (27 km) high and 340 miles (547 km) wide at its base. It grew this big because there are no tectonic plates on Mars, so magma bubbled up from a hot spot over billions of years.

CHAPTER 3

BURNING RING OF FIRE

Indonesia lies on the Ring of Fire, and Mount Bromo is one of its many volcanoes.

Mount Fuji in Japan, Mount Saint Helens in the United States, and Krakatoa in Indonesia are some of the world's most famous volcanoes. They all happen to be positioned around the fringes of the Pacific Ocean. They are not alone. Around 450 volcanoes are located in this area. As a result of the risk of eruptions and red-hot lava, this area is called the Ring of Fire.

Volcanic Horseshoe

The Ring of Fire is an incredibly large horseshoe in shape. In total, it measures 25,000 miles (40,234 km). It runs north from the base of Chile up to Alaska. It then turns south below Siberia, passing Japan, the Philippines, and finally, New Zealand. This is where the vast Pacific plate beneath the ocean meets several other tectonic plates underneath continents. These include the large North American and South American plates, the Eurasian plate, and the Australian and Filipino plates. The boundaries where these **continental plates** meet the Pacific **oceanic plate** are mostly **convergent boundaries**. Convergent plates are plates that are moving toward one another and pushing against or sliding over each other.

Why Here?

The Ring of Fire happens because the Pacific plate dips steeply beneath the land plates. This process is called subduction. Oceanic plates subduct because they are relatively denser, which means they have a heavier weight per volume of plate than continental plates. This is because they have been **compressed** by the weight of ocean water and also because the rock has absorbed water itself. The subducting plate heats up as it goes down into the mantle, and water boils off it to produce steam. This superheated steam helps produce more magma at the convergent boundary, so more volcanoes form.

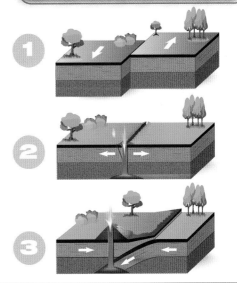

Plates slide from side to side at transform boundaries (1), pull apart at divergent boundaries (2), and dip under each other at convergent boundaries (3).

EARTH UNDER ATTACK!

The Ring of Fire is also home to around 80 percent of the earthquakes on our planet. Earthquakes happen when the jagged edges of plates at boundaries stick together. This builds a store of energy in plates that is released as shaking when the plates suddenly slip past each other. The tremors are so powerful that they can raze whole cities to the ground.

Will It Erupt?

Volcanoes can be divided into three categories based on their activity. Some are erupting right now, some might go off some time soon, and some have left their erupting days behind ... maybe!

Active Volcanoes

An active volcano is like a ticking time bomb. It will erupt whenever enough pressure has built up underground, out of sight. To be labeled active, a volcano has to have erupted in that last 2,500 years or so. Volcanologists estimate that there are currently around 1,900 active volcanoes. Some volcanoes are quiet for a long time between eruptions. However, given that our planet is nearly 4 billion years old, a few thousand years is a tiny gap between eruptions. Other volcanoes have been constantly active, with a sequence of eruptions over many years. These include the many volcanoes along the **mid-ocean ridges** that run deep under Earth's Pacific and Atlantic Oceans.

Anak Krakatau is an active volcano in Indonesia.

Mount Kilimanjaro is a famous and dormant volcano in Tanzania, East Africa.

Dormant or Extinct

Dormant volcanoes are those that have not been active for many thousands of years, according to geological records. For example, volcanologists **sample** rock around volcanic craters to test how old the erupted material is. However, any dormant volcano still has the potential to erupt again. That is because it is still located near plate boundaries or hot spots, and the processes in the mantle are ongoing. There are other volcanoes that volcanologists no longer consider a threat because the supply of magma to the surface is cut off. This can happen, for example, when a plate moves away from a hot spot. These are called extinct volcanoes.

EARTH UNDER ATTACK!

Mid-ocean ridges form where oceanic plates are always moving apart. At these divergent boundaries, magma always has space to get to the surface of the crust. The lava creates new crust, which builds up into high mountains. Some mountains are volcanoes from which lava periodically erupts.

Disaster Report: 2014, Ontake-san, Japan

On September 27, 2014, conditions could not have been better for climbing Ontake-san, Japan's second-biggest volcano after Mount Fuji. The leaves were just changing color as fall set in, the weather was beautiful, and it was a weekend, so many people had time off work to be outdoors.

Big Volcano

Ontake-san is more than 10,000 feet (3,048 m) tall and part of the Northern Alps mountain range on Japan's Honshu island. Ontake-san is easily reached by people living in the large cites of Nagoya and Nagano. Like other big mountains, hikers are keen to **summit** Ontake-san. It is also one of Japan's holy mountains and has been used for religious pilgrimages since 1792. There were no recorded historical eruptions at Ontake-san, and volcanologists knew it had been dormant for more than 300,000 years before some minor eruptions in 1979 and 2007. It was considered a safe volcano to climb.

Poisonous gases and smoke plumed from the peaks of Ontake-san for more than 2 weeks after the main eruption. The light gray areas on the center-left peaks are a coating of ash.

A view up the slopes to Ontake-san's summit minutes after its eruption shows the rapidly growing ash cloud.

Sudden Eruption

With no warning, Ontake-san erupted. Hikers taking photographs of the mountain suddenly noticed a fast-growing, enormous cloud of ash from the vent. High up on the mountain, many tried to run down trails, but the cloud caught up with them. The hot ash, poisonous gases, and rain of rocks fell on the fleeing people. Some hikers survived by distancing themselves from the summit and taking shelter in mountain lodges.

Aftermath

The eruption transformed the ancient temple and slopes of Ontake-san. Within minutes, the whole area was coated in gray ash. Rescue workers helped survivors who had difficulty breathing after being exposed to the ash, and they also collected the bodies of victims. Volcanologists tried to figure out what happened. Their network of scientific instruments on the mountain had registered no signs of eruption, such as movement of magma or shaking, on its slopes. They concluded that water must have seeped into the volcano and become superheated to form steam. The steam caused magma to rise and turn to ash in an instant.

DEADLY DATA   Ontake-san's eruption claimed the lives of 51 people.

CHAPTER 4

EYEWITNESS TO ERUPTIONS

Most eyewitnesses would agree that volcanic eruptions are astonishing and terrifying displays of the powerful forces within Earth. Eruptions can be sudden, but more often, there are signs beforehand that something bad is about to happen.

Changing Earth

Magma chambers filling up underground take up space. This pushes on the surrounding rock and can cause surface rock to push outward. Another change is in the gases. At vents of active volcanoes, there are usually gases escaping from underground. The gases are normally **dissolved** in magma but are released as magma nears the surface. They include steam and harmful or poisonous gases, such as sulfur dioxide and hydrogen sulfide. The places where gases escape are called fumaroles. Before an eruption, more gases may be released. The gases sometimes change the color of water in lakes or ponds.

Explosion!

The eruption of a volcano can be gentle when there is less trapped gas underground and runnier magma. Then streams of lava pour from the vent. When there is sticky magma and a lot of gas under pressure trapped inside, eruptions can produce some of the most dramatic explosions on the planet. They can blast lava, rocks, and ash tens of thousands of feet into the air. The sound can be deafening and is heard a long way away. For example, the eruption of Krakatoa, Indonesia, in 1883, was heard in Africa, around 3,000 miles (4,828 km) away and 4 hours after the actual explosion.

Yellow sulfur crystals growing around some volcanic vents are a sign that poisonous sulfurous gases are escaping from underground.

DEADLY DATA

Volcanologists measure eruptions by how much material, including magma, rock, and ash, is released. The Volcano Explosivity Index (VEI) grades eruptions from 1 to 8. Mount St. Helens' explosion in 1980 released 0.2 cubic miles (1 cubic km) of material and was rated VEI 5. This is tiny compared to Toba, Indonesia, which erupted 73,000 years ago. It released 240 cubic miles (1,000 cubic km) of material, rating it a maximum VEI 8.

Different Eruptions

Volcanoes are unpredictable. No two eruptions are exactly the same, and each one can produce a range of terrifying effects. This is partly to do with what type of lava is involved.

This **fire fountain** is erupting from Mount Etna, Italy, with the lights of the nearby city of Catania in the background.

Lava

Lava fresh from underground is usually 1,292 to 2,192° Fahrenheit (700–1,200° C). That is nearly three times as hot as a pizza oven. The lava glows white or red-hot. It is slow to cool and harden into gray rock, especially deeper lava flows. Some lava forms a smooth, wrinkly crust on top as it cools, but other lava has a rougher texture. The stickiness of lava depends on what chemicals it contains: The stickiest usually contain a lot of **silica**.

Fire Fountains and Eruption Columns

Fire fountains happen when very fluid lava shoots skyward like fireworks. The jets of lava can keep spurting for days and are most dramatic when seen at night. Some fire fountains can reach heights of hundreds of feet. The lava can pour off slopes, or on flat volcanoes, it can pile up into **spatter cones** where it lands. Some eruptions happen when the top of a vent or crater fills with magma, and rising bubbles of gas pop, sending out bursts of lava skyward at intervals. The most explosive volcanic events can create **eruption columns**. These happen when the force of a blast turns magma into tall, vertical clouds of ash that stretch up to 35 miles (56 km) high.

Deadly Flow

The most deadly eruptions are pyroclastic flows. These happen when a mix of hot gases and steam lift up ash and chunks of lava into a kind of airborne **avalanche**. The pyroclastic flow can move faster than the winds in a hurricane, at up to 600 feet per second (183 m/s). They move fastest down the steepest slopes, such as deep valleys, and can travel up to 125 miles (201 km).

EARTH UNDER ATTACK!

Pyroclastic flows are sometimes called *nuées ardentes*, which means "glowing clouds." They are so named because the hot gases and ash burn red-hot at temperatures of hundreds of degrees Fahrenheit. These terrible clouds burn everything in their path.

Some sticky, silica-rich lava wrinkles and piles up into rope shapes as it cools.

Volcanic Hazards

Volcanoes create a lot of very dangerous materials in addition to blisteringly hot lava. These include hot, poisonous gases and ash that can cause eye and throat problems, burns, lung damage, and death.

Lahars

Sometimes, the ash and larger fragments of volcanic **debris** with small holes can become soaked with water, forming a kind of volcanic mud. On a slope, this mud can then become wet and heavy enough to slide downhill like an avalanche. This is called a lahar. The lahar is very heavy and unstoppable. When it comes to rest, the particles push together, and the water drains away, so it can set like concrete. Anything it has covered is trapped and set in stone.

The path of destruction by a recent lahar from Tunguragua volcano, Ecuador, is clear in this valley.

Volcanic bombs are blasted upward as searing lava and fall as hard rock.

Other Natural Disasters

Eruptions can also cause other natural disasters. The heat of lava or pyroclastic flows can melt and dislodge vast chunks of ice from glaciers or break away snow fields from slopes, causing avalanches. These can be as devastating as lahars. The collapse of the side of a volcano during an eruption, a vast pyroclastic flow, or a giant underwater eruption can also cause **tsunamis**. The change in the height of the sea floor starts waves that grow taller and taller as they reach other shores. Tsunamis can destroy coastlines through their powerful wave forces and also flood the land.

EARTH UNDER ATTACK!

The materials ejected by volcanic explosions include bombs that start off as lumps of lava. Some bombs elongate, or stretch, as they fly quickly through the air and cool. Others land and flatten like cow pies. Regardless of the shape, these falling chunks of heavy rock can cause great damage. **Pumice**, however, is less of a problem. This rock is very light and looks like sponge. That is because it is full of holes formed by volcanic gases escaping through lava.

Disaster Report: 1997, Soufriere Hills, Montserrat

Montserrat is a lush island in the West Indies. It is surrounded by warm, turquoise sea. It has steep slopes, including the Silver Hill in the north, the Centre Hills, and the Soufriere Hills in the south. These volcanoes formed in ancient times. Montserrat is on the Ring of Fire, but its volcanoes were all considered to be dormant. That is, until the 1990s, when the Soufriere Hills came to life.

Buildup

Chances Peak, an area of Soufriere, has a lot of old lava domes. There, in 1992, volcanologists detected several weak earthquakes. In 1995, there was further ground shaking and the first eruptions on Montserrat for 500 years. Ash spewing from a lava dome proved that the volcano was now active. The government **evacuated** approximately 5,000 people from the southern half of the island near the volcano. These were mostly from the capital, Plymouth, located just 3 miles (4.8 km) away from the eruption.

A giant pyroclastic flow races down the slopes of the Soufriere Hills.

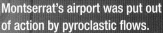
Montserrat's airport was put out of action by pyroclastic flows.

Collapse

Volcanologists monitored changes at Chances Peak. The most worrying was a new lava dome bulging out at the top. When this cracked, it sent boulders tumbling down the slopes. Then, in June, the dome's weight caused it to collapse into the vent. This shattered the searing rock and magma into catastrophic pyroclastic flows, which affected much of the southern half of the island. It killed 19 people, who had returned to their homes against advice in order to raise crops. The pyroclastic flow from the collapse of another new dome in August destroyed Plymouth and the island's airport. Eruptions have continued up to the present day.

EARTH UNDER ATTACK!

An eruption of Chance's Peak in 1996 caused a large pyroclastic flow that sped down the valley of the Tar River into the sea. Here, the material in the flow created a new fan-shaped platform of land jutting out from the coast.

CHAPTER 5

VOLCANIC IMPACTS

The heat, ash, and burning lava of a volcano leaves a wave of destruction in its path. Like any other natural disaster, volcanoes can totally transform lives and places within minutes or hours. For the unluckiest people, volcanoes mean injury or even death. However, even those lucky enough to escape an active volcano may face a very different future.

Disaster Strikes

A volcano can bury towns and villages under a dense blanket of ash. When tons of ash fall at the same time, buildings can collapse. The problem becomes worse if rain falls because the rain soaks the ash and makes it heavier. This causes more collapses. Volcanoes can start avalanches that envelop people and places in heavy snow. Lahars can flatten forests, choke rivers, and crush buildings. Burning rocks exploded from the volcano's fracture drop from the sky and can set trees and buildings ablaze. The air is filled with dust and ash, making it hard for people to see where they are going. The ash and dust may also cause breathing problems. Wind can spread clouds of ash and dust over a wide area, polluting the air for miles around.

Escape

Firefighters are often the first of the emergency services to arrive on the scene when a volcano strikes. They brave the intense heat and danger to put out the fires and clear the way for people to escape from the area. Volcanoes can erupt several times in a row, so it is vital for survivors to evacuate the area as fast as they can. Sometimes, lava flows cut off roads and bridges, making it hard for people to escape. The heat from the ash, steam, and lava can even melt roads and buckle bridges, cutting off escape routes.

People escaping volcanoes after eruptions may face the hazard of falling, choking, and cloaking ash.

DEADLY DATA

In 1985 in Colombia, South America, a once-dormant volcano exploded into life, spewing hot ash that melted ice and snow. The mix of ash, soil, and water created a mudflow that buried an entire town and flooded others, killing more than 22,500 people.

Search and Rescue

As soon as a disaster like a volcanic eruption happens, teams of search-and-rescue workers spring into action. Every minute counts because victims must be found as quickly as possible. People may be suffering life-threatening injuries or trapped under collapsed buildings where air supplies are limited. The sooner victims are found, rescued, and taken to safety and medical care, the better their chances of survival.

Search Techniques

There is a range of ways to find victims. One simple way is for specially trained dogs to sniff out people buried under collapsed buildings, ash, or rubble. A more complicated way involves using the latest **radar** technology, such as FINDER. FINDER is designed to detect heartbeats of victims trapped in wreckage. It sends a low-powered microwave signal, about one-thousandth of a cell phone's output, through rubble and even thick concrete, and detects changes in those signals when they reflect back from tiny movements caused by victims' breathing and heartbeats.

Advancing lava can ruin settlements, leaving buildings, fields, and roads trapped among new rock.

Mountain Rescue

Every year, millions of people climb mountains formed from volcanoes that are still designated as active. If one of these suddenly erupts without any warning, it can impact hundreds of people staying in lodges or hiking on the slopes of the volcano. They may be buried in ash or trapped in buildings. To reach high slopes quickly, rescue teams have to fly there in helicopters and be lowered to the ground. Victims may be airlifted to safety and flown to nearby hospitals.

Helicopters are often the only way to reach people trapped or injured by eruptions high in remote mountainous areas.

EARTH UNDER ATTACK!

Rescue work is risky, and search and rescue teams not only need to be brave, but they must also be trained to spot signs of danger. In places, the lava forms a crust that looks solid and is cool, but it can easily break. Beneath it, there may be molten, burning lava. There is also always a risk the volcano may erupt at any time.

Ongoing Issues

After the eruption of Mount Merapi, Indonesia, in 2010, exhausted survivors took shelter in public buildings after fleeing the danger zone.

After people have evacuated the danger zone and the last survivors have been plucked from danger and delivered to safety, there is much work to do. People who have been forced to evacuate their homes need somewhere to stay. They also need food, water, medical treatment, and comfort.

Help at Hand

Volunteers, government workers, and aid organizations, such as the International Red Cross, get to work. They transport people to places where they can stay, such as school gymnasiums. They provide survivors with first aid, bedding, food, and drink. They also offer people things like books and games, which can help fill the hours they spend waiting before they can travel to stay with families or find alternative housing. Some workers are counselors that are trained to help people talk about their fears and other feelings. Talking about the volcano may help survivors recover from the trauma of the volcano disaster.

Aid Work

Aid agencies are especially important in poorer countries where volcanoes can destroy all the fields and farm crops that families rely on to survive. In countries like these, aid workers give out food parcels, and they set up shelters and tents, where people can sleep safely and warmly. They also use innovative ways to provide relief. For example, one mass text-message program allows aid workers to identify all the cell phones being used in a given area. It then sends them urgent updates about things such as **sanitation** and medical aid at the click of a button.

EARTH UNDER ATTACK!

Aid efforts can sometimes be interrupted by the effects of the volcano. Aircraft flights can be interrupted after a volcano fills the air with eruption columns and clouds of ash and dust. This makes it impossible for other countries to provide help by delivering food and other supplies by air.

Flights were canceled across Europe for over a week in 2010 after the eruption of Eyjafjallajokull in Iceland. This is because erupted ash in the atmosphere could have damaged aircraft engines.

Moving On

A volcano can cause sweeping changes to an area of countryside or whole towns and cities. After an eruption is finally over and before people can move back to their homes, massive cleanup operations are usually necessary.

Cleaning up fine, blanketing ash after a volcanic eruption can be a difficult and time-consuming task.

Cleaning Up

Among the worst things that volcanoes leave behind are the vast, sprawling piles of ash. Bulldozers and trucks remove rubble and rocks, but removing, transporting, and disposing of volcanic ash is an especially dirty, time-consuming, and expensive task. Wind can stir and billow fine particles of ash into the air, even dropping it onto areas that have just been cleaned. Sweepers, water-spraying vehicles, and people with shovels wearing overalls and breathing masks, work quickly to remove it. In places where ash sets like a carpet of gray concrete, it can take years to clear an area using hammer drills and bulldozers.

This is what can happen to the inside of a house when it is in the path of a pyroclastic flow.

Rebuilding Lives

When streets and areas are cleared of ash and rubble, workers check that buildings are safe to enter. They then start to repair or rebuild those that are damaged or destroyed. People also need help restarting their businesses. For example, in poorer countries, where farms have been devastated, governments and aid agencies may supply families with seeds and tools, so that they can start farming and feeding themselves again. Farmers may need new supplies of livestock to replace animals killed in the eruption. Roads may also need to be rebuilt. The total cost of rebuilding lives after a severe volcano can be enormous.

DEADLY DATA

After a mighty volcano erupted in Mount St. Helens in Skamania County, Washington, on May 18, 1980, the area was transformed. It took the US Army Corps of Engineers months to shift almost 1 million tons (0.9 mt) of ash from nearby roads to disused quarries. It took 600 trips for trucks to clear away the trees destroyed by the blast. Altogether, it cost more than $1 billion to complete the cleanup operation.

CHAPTER 6

LIVING WITH VOLCANOES

Imagine living in the shadow of a volcano and all those possible hazards when it erupts! Why would you stay there? Amazingly, more than 300 million people live in volcanically active areas. There are many reasons why they stay there.

Soil Story

Lava, ash, and rock from eruptions gradually weather, or break down, over time. This happens by the action of water, sunshine, and wind. The weathering releases chemical **nutrients** from rocks, which can be taken up by plants. Nutrients help plants grow quickly and healthily, and they also help store moisture in soil. Farmers grow successful crops on volcanic slopes with well-weathered volcanic soil. For example, tomatoes, grapes, and orange trees grow abundantly on the slopes around Mount Etna, in Italy. Important New Zealand **export** products, such as kiwi fruits, come mostly from volcanic soils.

Precious Minerals

Gold, silver, and copper are some of the precious **minerals** found near volcanoes. Rising magma cooling and hardening beneath the volcano is the source for these minerals. Superhot water circulates through the magma and dissolves the metals from it. The metals are **deposited** in cracks nearer the surface when the solution cools. Miners search around volcanoes for these precious minerals.

Grape vines grow well in mineral-rich volcanic soil on the island of Lanzarote, Canary Islands, Spain.

Heat Energy

The heat from magma near the surface is an excellent source of energy. Geothermal energy uses this natural heat of Earth to warm homes or make electricity. At geothermal power plants, water is pumped deep underground where it is boiled before being pumped back to the surface. The hot steam turns machines called generators, which produce electricity. The hot water is also pumped to heat buildings and swimming pools.

EARTH UNDER ATTACK!

Volcanoes are destructive but also constructive. More than 80 percent of the rock surface of our planet was created by volcanic eruptions. Eruptions from ancient volcanoes billions of years ago gave off gases that helped make the atmosphere suitable for breathing by animals, including people.

Predicting Volcanoes

Just as it is difficult to get weather forecasts exactly right, so it is tricky to predict volcanic eruptions accurately. However, volcanologists do have a number of ways to help their predictions.

Looking at History

Volcanologists study survivor's accounts of past eruptions. They take samples of rock from the area around volcanoes. Samples can show when ancient eruptions happened and what they were like. For example, were they lava eruptions or pyroclastic flows? This historical record can give clues about what future eruptions might be like.

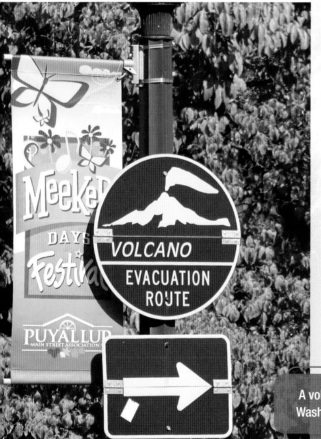

Looking Underground

Seismology is the study of seismic waves. Seismic waves are vibrations that happen when Earth's plates clash. They can be detected miles from plate boundaries because the waves travel through rock like ripples across a pond. Volcanologists set up sensitive instruments called seismometers. These contain a weight held in place by springs. The way the weight swings changes with the size, direction, and speed of seismic waves. Stronger, faster seismic waves can precede an eruption.

A volcano evacuation route is signposted in Washington State, which is on the Ring of Fire.

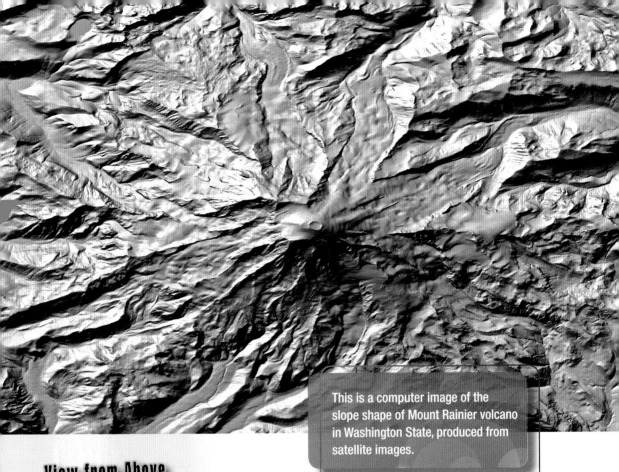

This is a computer image of the slope shape of Mount Rainier volcano in Washington State, produced from satellite images.

View from Above

Volcanologists also use **satellites** to help with their predictions. Satellites carry instruments that can help study our planet. Some cameras can detect new plumes of ash from volcanoes, while others can capture images of air temperature in the atmosphere. The air often gets warmer above active volcanoes. Radar instruments send radio signals from satellites to Earth's surface, which bounce back to space. When a volcano bulges because of magma collecting underneath, the time for the bounce slightly decreases, helping scientists to predict an eruption.

EARTH UNDER ATTACK!

Volcano predictions help authorities plan for a worst-case scenario. They make hazard maps showing where people are at risk from eruptions. They get emergency services to train staff in how to help after an eruption, such as knowing how to treat expected injuries. Authorities work out evacuation plans, including safest routes and where to find emergency food, water, and shelters.

Up Close

Taking measurements from afar is helpful in predicting and knowing more about eruptions. However, sometimes there is no substitute for getting up close and personal with a volcano.

A volcanologist protects his hands with heatproof gloves as he collects lava samples.

Getting Samples

Volcanologists must wear special equipment before taking samples from lava flows and vents. They put on goggles, breathing masks, heatproof clothing, and other safety gear. The places they are going are among the most extreme on our planet, so there is a very real danger of being exposed to poisonous gases, burning lava, and other hazards. They take samples of blobs of lava at the end of long poles. Some cool quickly, but they must dip other, hotter samples quickly in water, so that they do not change chemically in the air as they cool very slowly. Volcanologists also sample gases by using machines with sensors that work like noses to detect the chemicals in air. Sometimes these are mounted on drones, or flying robots, which volcanologists can fly inside a vent without endangering themselves too much. The drones can take pictures and measure temperatures, too.

Seeing Smoke

It is very dangerous to get close to eruption clouds, but volcanologists can learn about the gases they contain from a safe distance. They can use a device called a COSPEC. This can detect how natural light shining through the plume of smoke from a volcano differs from the same light shining through clear air. It can detect the type of gas and how much of it is emerging from the vent each day.

EARTH UNDER ATTACK!

Volcanologists study lava samples in specially equipped labs. They use powerful machines to crush and twist lava to calculate the forces needed to make it shatter and bend. They use devices to heat lava until it melts, so that they can study the chemicals it contains. All of this data can help volcanologists understand the deadly processes that occur during an eruption.

Webcams set up at Kilauea volcano, Hawaii, are used to record and transmit images to computers in volcanology labs where scientists can monitor and study changes, such as emerging smoke.

Disaster Report:
2016, Tungurahua, Ecuador

Tungurahua is one of the most active volcanoes on Earth. This cauldron-like crater in Ecuador has been bubbling away for years, with quiet periods of several years when it has been inactive, followed by small to moderate eruptions. In 2016, there was a more explosive event.

Fiery Light Show

In March 2016, columns of ash spewed out of the top of Tungurahua that reached 23,000 feet (7,000 m) into the air. Volcanologists counted at least 70 substantial explosions. The volcano gave off a dramatic, fiery light show, which also resulted in a dusting of ash across the region, pyroclastic flows, and the ejection of blocks of glowing, burning volcanic rock that landed on the ground up to 1 mile (1.6 km) away. Volcanologists fear that this moderate eruption may be a precursor to something much bigger and more dangerous.

A giant ash cloud rose from Tungurahua Volcano, Ecuador, in 2016. Could this be just the dress rehearsal for a major eruption?

The town of Banos nestles in a valley beneath Tungurahua's slopes and is at risk from pyroclastic flows, lahars, and other volcanic hazards if a major eruption occurs.

Throat of Fire

In the local Quechua language, *Tungurahu* means "throat of fire," and this volcano is constantly active and erupting. It is under constant monitoring by volcanologists, who believe it may erupt violently again in the near future. Monitoring stations have recorded that the volcano is steadily swelling, which is very possibly a sign that new magma is building up below the surface. The volcano's last big eruption happened between 1916 and 1918, and if a similar eruption happens in the future, it could be disastrous. Therefore, the region is on alert, and many people have temporarily abandoned their homes and are staying away from the area. Evacuation routes are marked with green arrows throughout the nearby tourist town of Banos.

DEADLY DATA

Tungurahua is situated about 85 miles (140 km) south of Quito, Ecuador's populous capital city, and it overlooks the tourist town of Banos. The volcano is 16,475 feet (5,023 m) high and has been erupting on and off since 1999.

Future Volcanoes

Volcanologists are constantly being asked where the next big eruption is about to happen. They know that wherever there is a supply of rising magma, there could be a volcano. However, improving technology and building better networks of sensing equipment should help us predict eruptions.

The Next Big One?

Some of the possible candidates include Mount Vesuvius in Italy and Krakatoa in Indonesia. Both are famous for the impacts of their biggest eruptions. Another is Yellowstone Caldera in Yellowstone National Park in Wyoming. This natural tourist attraction sits on top of a **supervolcano** tens of miles across. When Yellowstone Caldera last erupted violently 640,000 years ago, it blanketed most of North America in thick ash. Volcanologists think there is enough magma beneath it to fill up the Grand Canyon 11 times! Just imagine the havoc that could cause to the continent.

The many walkers and climbers visiting Mount Rainier each year need to be aware that this volcano could erupt at any time.

Mexico City and surrounding suburbs are home to 20 million people living in the shadow of Popocatepetl volcano. This volcano has had 15 major eruptions since the sixteenth century.

Volcanoes and Climate

The giant eruption of Mount Pinatubo in the Philippines sent around 20 million tons (18 million mt) of sulfur dioxide into the atmosphere. This had the effect of reflecting more of the sun's warmth than usual back into space. The impact was a worldwide drop in temperature and shifting patterns of rainfall in Asia. There are many other examples of eruptions changing **climate**. Other gases released in eruptions, such as carbon dioxide, trap heat, increasing average global temperature. This process is called global warming. Most scientists agree that people cause much more global warming than volcanoes because machines, such as power plants and airplanes, release carbon dioxide when they burn fuel. This helps remind us that while we need to monitor volcanic activity, we also need to monitor our own human actions on Earth.

EARTH UNDER ATTACK!

Some scientists believe that human activity could cause eruptions. People sometimes pump wastewater deep underground to get rid of it. They may pump fluids into deep **oil wells** to wash out the oil from holes in the rock. These liquids might cause plates to shift and magma to rise.

GLOSSARY

avalanche when snow or ice slips down a slope

climate the usual pattern of weather that happens in a place

compressed pressed together

continental plates tectonic plates underlying a landmass

convergent boundaries where two tectonic plates move together

debris fragments left after something has been destroyed

dense closely packed

deposited laid down in a specific place

dissolved mixed completely with a liquid

eruption columns types of eruption when a cloud of ash and dust rises high into the atmosphere

evacuated moved away from an area that is dangerous to somewhere that is safe

export to send to other countries for profit

fire fountain a type of eruption when lava shoots upward like a fountain

lava domes volcanoes where sticky lava builds up into a rounded lump above a vent

magma hot, liquid rock below the surface of Earth

mid-ocean ridges long underwater mountain ranges formed where tectonic plates move apart

minerals substances in nature that do not come from living things

mudflow an avalanche of mud

nutrients substances that living things need to grow and be healthy

oceanic plate tectonic plate underlying an ocean

oil wells holes drilled to access oil trapped naturally in rocks underground

pressure pushing force

pumice a very lightweight type of volcanic rock

quarries places where stone, gravel, or other materials are dug up

radar a way of finding the position of an object by bouncing a radio wave off it and analyzing the reflected wave

sample to take a part from a larger item or group to test

sanitation supply of clean water and hygienic disposal of waste

satellites objects in space often used for helping communications on Earth by passing on information

silica hard mixture of chemicals often found at Earth's surface as sand or quartz rock

spatter cones small, steep volcano cone formed from mini eruptions of lava blobs

summit to reach the top of a mountain

superheated heated up past its boiling temperature

supervolcano a volcano capable of ejecting more than 240 cubic miles (1,000 cubic km) of material

tsunamis huge sea waves caused by a shift in the height of the seafloor

FOR MORE INFORMATION

BOOKS

Collins editors. *Earthquakes and Volcanoes* (Collins Fascinating Facts).
New York, NY: HarperCollins, 2016.

DK editors. *Volcanoes* (DK findout!). New York, NY: Dorling Kindersely, 2016.

Reynolds, Shaye. *Volcanoes* (Spotlight on Earth Science). New York, NY:
PowerKids Press, 2017.

Schuh, Mari C. *Volcanoes* (Earth in Action). Mankato, Minnesota:
Capstone Press, 2016.

WEBSITES

Get more facts about volcanoes at:
www.ready.gov/kids/know-the-facts/volcano

Find instructions to make your own volcano eruption at:
volcano.oregonstate.edu/kids

Explore some of the worst volcanic disasters of the past 400 years at:
www.pbs.org/wgbh/nova/earth/deadly-volcanoes.html

Follow the eruption story of Mount Vesuvius at:
**www.britishmuseum.org/whats_on/exhibitions/pompeii_and_
herculaneum/pompeii_live/eruption_timeline.aspx**

Visit this interactive guide about volcanoes at:
www.dkfindout.com/us/earth/volcanoes

Publisher's note to educators and parents: Our editors have carefully reviewed these websites to ensure that they are suitable for students. Many websites change frequently, however, and we cannot guarantee that a site's future contents will continue to meet our high standards of quality and educational value. Be advised that students should be closely supervised whenever they access the Internet.

INDEX